Phonicability Games

VERA CONWAY

MAGIC 'E'

HOPSCOTCH PUBLISHING

MAGIC 'E'

Phonicability Games

Phonicability Games

CONTENTS

Published by Hopscotch Educational Publishing Ltd,
29 Waterloo Place, Leamington Spa CV32 5LA
(Tel: 01926 744227)

© 2002 Hopscotch Educational Publishing

Written by Vera Conway
Series design by Blade Communications
Illustrated by Dave Burroughs
Printed by Clintplan, Southam

ISBN 1-904307-17-5

Introduction

The idea of inventing games of this nature was first conceived out of sheer desperation when I met my first uncooperative pupil. He told me confidently, 'I do not need to learn to read because I am going to be an actor.' As he was then only seven years old and quite unable to project his mind into the future, no argument of mine could convince him to believe otherwise.

A year later when this boy was diagnosed as being severely dyslexic he was triumphant. He stubbornly closed his mind to everyone's attempts to help him and his behaviour in school gave much cause for concern, but our lessons continued. I spent two hours with him each week and, in spite of himself, he learned to read and write. The almost-miracle was achieved by means of games we played together, which he actually enjoyed.

Since then, every game in this series has been played time and time again with people who have a variety of problems as well as with those who appear to learn to read and write without experiencing any difficulties. As I saw more and more people benefiting from playing the games, I wanted to share them with others – both old and young – so that they could experience the joy and laughter that come with learning to read and spell. I hope, also, that teachers, parent teachers and helpers of all kinds will become better acquainted with the simple logic of teaching reading and spelling by phonics (sounds).

This is by no means a return to something old-fashioned in a back-to-basics approach. We are all discovering the real worth of a teaching method which, speaking generally, has not been profoundly comprehended. Nor has it been widely appreciated, so the subject could not have been taught effectively in the past. Fortunately, things are changing now; the extensive illiteracy throughout English-speaking countries has excited much research. This adds authenticity to many small, enlightening experiments and discoveries currently being made by the few teachers who have the courage to probe. We are finding not only that it is pleasurable to teach reading and spelling by phonics, but also that hardly any pupils need to fail to learn to read.

I use these games in conjunction with Mrs Violet Brand's scheme, using the order in which the sounds are introduced in *SAM* (Egon). Each game supports and extends the new steps within the structure of the scheme, but they can be played in any order.

The games are unbelievably simple and, in principle, well within the capabilities of every potential reader. Significant progress is currently being realised by a ten-year-old boy who experienced boredom and failure; the games have revitalised his reading lessons. A girl aged eleven who spoke a dialect could not order the alphabet and despaired of ever learning to read. She now reads simple texts and plays the games with enjoyment.

Each game either practises and reinforces the sound/symbol relationship that has just been taught or introduces the pupil to the next one. Some games combine these two aims. When the games are presented to the pupil at the optimum moments in his reading development, newly learned rules are established. (NB We have used 'he' throughout this book to refer to the pupil. This is done purely for the purposes of consistency and clarity. It is not intended to imply that males have more problems with reading than females. In other books in the series we use 'she' throughout.)

Although these games can help any pupil to learn to read and spell, they have proved to be particularly useful and effective for pupils who have experienced years of failure in most of their school subjects because of their poor reading skills. One eight-year-old boy who was sent to me to receive 'help' draped himself over the back of his chair as we began the first lesson and refused to look at anything on the table. Learning to read had become anathema to him; he had received plenty of 'help', but he still couldn't read and so he had given up trying. His reaction presented a tense moment for me; I did not know him and I certainly did not want to spoil our relationship before it had even begun! I took out a game and shook the dice. 'Look, Perry,' I said. 'I am playing a game, and I am winning.' Fortunately, he won… and gladly came again.

Success in winning the games does not depend on a pupil's ability to read or spell. The real secret of success lies in the fact that, quite subtly, the learning/teaching element is relegated to second place in favour of 'luck'. Because of this, pupils do not feel anxious when they play. There are no worries or tensions; they are confident that they **can** tackle something that appears to be so easy. In such a relaxed atmosphere, they can enjoy the fun of playing and even the triumph of beating the teacher! This latter achievement boosts the confidence of almost every pupil and it is very important to them. I have heard little ones discussing the play later in the day and looking very pleased with themselves as they've said, 'I won two games today.'

On the other hand, if the pupil loses, he can experience losing a game respectably, without any sense of failure, since he knows that he lost because the dice did not fall in his favour and definitely not because he was stupid!

Teachers will not, of course, be trying to win! On the contrary, and especially with younger children or those whose confidence needs to be built up, the teacher will contrive to lose the game! He or she will soon learn subtle ways to lose, by forgetting where the winning card is, by missing a turn, by always allowing the pupil to go first at the beginning of play, by working out whose will be the last card and by making helpful suggestions to the pupil so that he gets the advantage. I have also even turned a blind eye to a little cheating that works towards my purpose. Players have to know what they are doing in order to cheat... but of course I make it very clear that I do not approve of cheating and I correct it when I 'see' it!

Each game has its own very clear aim about which part of the reading structure it supports. There are, however, some subsidiary aims that make the games even more valuable; look out for these as you play.

ASSESSMENT

This is sometimes, for me, the main reason for playing a game. I often need to assess how much of the new work the pupil has assimilated and whether or not he is ready to go on. I assess the situation continually as I watch his strategies as he plays the game. I 'listen' to his thinking processes and to the use he makes of the sounds in the words. I need to know if he is really hearing the sounds or travelling down the dead-end road of remembering the words in 'look and say' fashion. If the latter is true, I know that more practice, more patient explanation and more adaptation to approach the problem from a different angle are all needed. During every game, I have to learn when to wait patiently for the pupil to remember and when to intervene with reassuring help. Playing these games has, in fact, helped me to be able to assess more precisely where the pupil is in his progress and how to help him move on.

VOCABULARY

Each of these games extends the pupils' spoken vocabulary as well as helping them to read and spell. I always talk to them about the words we are using, about the meanings of the words and how they fit into sentences. I have been surprised by the number of pupils who do not know how to use some of the simple, three-letter words such as 'tub', 'wig', 'den' and 'pan', let alone the more difficult ones. I encourage the children to give clear definitions of the words to help them to remember when they later need to read them and use them in their own compositions.

MEMORY TRAINING

Memory training is intrinsic to many of the games and with some ingenuity on the part of the teacher even more use can be made of the games to help pupils remember than might at first be apparent. I often ask questions while we are playing, such as 'Where is the elephant?' or 'If we add a magic "e" to hot, what happens?' (It makes a word that we can say but is not a real word to be found in a dictionary.) The most difficult part of learning to spell is remembering which symbol to use from the selection that represents the same sound: 'ai', 'ay', 'a-e' for example. Should 'rain' be spelled 'rane', 'rayne' or 'rain'? The games most certainly help to sort out problems of this kind.

As you become more familiar with the games, countless opportunities will occur to you to use the materials to test pupils' memory skills.

CONCLUSION

It has been my intention to make the games simple, attractive and fun to play. I have borne in mind, too, that they need to be played in a short time because I know from experience how little time many teachers have to spend with individual pupils.

I hope that the games can be photocopied cheaply so that copies may be taken home. Younger pupils especially like to share what they have enjoyed with their families and the additional practice will be good for them. Alternatively, sets of games can be made up and stored as a resource, which can be lent to parents and returned.

The clear aims and simple rules help parents to become effective teachers who, in turn, can give valuable help in playing the games with other pupils. The components of the games may also be used as a resource to illustrate specific teaching points. I have used the games in this way with older pupils who do not necessarily need the competitive approach.

The pictures will also inspire many useful worksheets and ideas for new games, so there are many uses for these photocopiable materials.

PLAYING THE GAMES

Most of the games are designed for two players who can either be the pupil and the teacher or two pupils playing together with the teacher or competent adult as referee. All reading games need supervision and mine are no exception, but the simplicity of these enables parents and classroom helpers to grasp the principles quickly to support the work of the teacher.

The rules of these games are very flexible and can be modified by the teacher to suit the pupil. Pupils sometimes change the rules and I have been happy to allow them to do that provided that the game is still fair and the main aims are accomplished.

There is a great deal of repetition of the rules across the selection of games. This aids each pupil's confidence and allows them to concentrate on the main purpose of the game without having to contend with more complicated instructions.

Pupils should move through the scheme at their own pace and teachers will find that there are more games for those sound/symbol groups that need most practice. Not all pupils need to play all of the games. Teachers need to be aware of individual pupils' needs. There is little to be gained from playing a game once a pupil has understood that step, except, perhaps, to boost his confidence.

Teachers and helpers need to make sure that pupils know what the pictures represent before the game begins. Such a preview lends opportunity to talk about words and pictures and is an important part of the learning process.

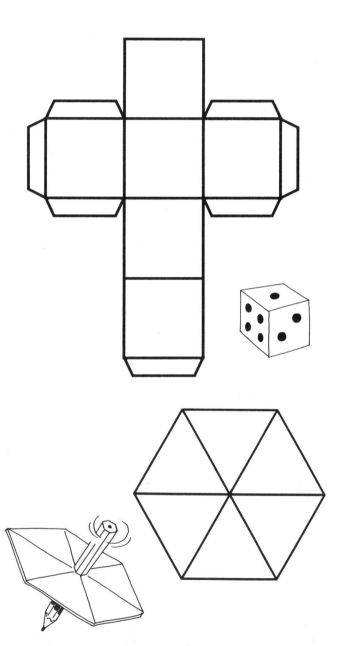

HOW TO MAKE THE GAMES

○ Photocopy the required pages according to the instructions for each game, enlarging or reducing as you prefer. I made all my games to fit into zipped reading book folders measuring 40 x 27cm. This helps to keep the weight down when I have to carry a selection of games to school.

○ Colour the pictures; I have found coloured pencils to be the best tools to use. Enlist the help of anyone who is willing, but if you intend to make your games permanent, make sure that your 'colourers' have high standards.

○ Cut up the sheets as instructed and mount the pieces and the boards on card using an adhesive.

○ If you intend to cover your games with Tacky Back, (and this will certainly preserve them for much use in the future) then use water-based ink pens. Spirit-based ink spreads under Tacky Back. You may prefer to mount the games on thinner card and laminate them.

EXTRA EQUIPMENT REQUIRED

○ Nearly all of the games can be played in a shorter time, if necessary, so I find it useful to carry an egg-timer in my bag.

○ Blank dice can be obtained from:
Taskmaster Ltd, Morris Road, Leicester LE2 6BR

○ Make your feely bags from attractive pieces of material. Cut out a rectangle that is just a little longer than an A4 sheet of paper. Stitch the sides and hem the top. Thread a string through if you wish.

○ Buttons can be used for counters, or you can buy some from Taskmaster (see previous column). For 'counters' to move on the board, I collect trinkets or small toys from cereal packets. All these little novelties help to make the games more attractive.

○ Stock up with zipped reading book folders for simple storage. I label my folders with my own description of the contents so that I can find the game I need quickly. I also put a mounted copy of the rules for the game into the folder with the pieces.

○ Patience! – You will need much patience, too. If you have a will to teach reading, patience grows with the thrill of achievement in both pupil and teacher. I trust that these little games will bring much satisfaction to many people.

An emergency dice or spinner can be made using the pattern opposite. You can enlarge or reduce it according to your needs.

Using this Book

Magic 'e'; fairy 'e'; powerful 'e'; silent 'e'; whatever you choose to call it, there is no way round the fact that the silent 'e' letter in English words causes much confusion amongst those who are learning to read and spell. All pupils will benefit from having teachers who understand the difficulties and are able to explain the simple but important rules regarding the letter, in a logical manner.

The sounds for which 'c' and 'g' stand, usually as in 'cat' and 'goat' are altered when the letters are followed by 'e' (or 'i' or 'y'). 'c' then stands for the 's' sound, as in 'ice', 'nice', 'grace', 'place', and the 'g' sounds like 'j' in 'page', 'huge', 'pigeon'. Silent 'e' completes such words as 'have', 'love', 'glove', because no English word ends with a 'v'.

The silent 'e' that appears on the ends of words such as 'house', 'mouse', 'horse', 'please' and 'promise' seems to have no known purpose except to 'stick the "s" on' to whole words without suffixes that end with one 's', but are not plural. That still leaves words like 'some', 'come' and 'none', with 'e's for which there seems to be no explanation, except perhaps an historical one. Silent 'e' also provides the necessary vowel in the second syllable of words with an 'le' ending, such as 'candle', 'kettle', 'whistle', 'table'. All syllables must have a vowel.

The games in this book are, however, concerned with that 'magical' quality of 'e' that works with vowels 'a', 'i', 'o' and 'u'. ('ee' is learned separately as the 'ee' sound is rarely separated by a consonant as it is in 'Eve', 'mete', 'here', 'theme', and 'these'. Games for the 'ee' sound are in the Digraphs book in this series.)

'e' working with vowels changes the spelling and meaning of some words – 'hat' becomes 'hate', 'pip' becomes 'pipe', for example, while for others it is vital for correct pronunciation and intelligibility. Pupils need to know that this kind of silent 'e' helps the vowel to stand for its name instead of its usual sound.

After pupils have been thoroughly drilled to recognise and use 'a' as the symbol for the sound in 'pan', for example (and for some pupils, learning the vowel sounds presents a great deal of difficulty), it is somewhat disconcerting for them to discover that when they see 'e' working with the vowel, they have to say the name of the vowel instead of the sound. I have found that, even though some pupils know the names of the vowels very well, they find this change hard to cope with at first. They have to learn to look very carefully for the magic 'e' when they are reading, and they are likely to pepper 'e's around indiscriminately in their written work until they have a better understanding of the function. The importance of the function of magic 'e' cannot be overstressed. Its influence continues even when it is not a part of the spelling of some words that the pupil will soon meet in his reading or need in his written work; 'sliding', 'smoking' and 'shining' are examples of this.

I believe that it is easy for the teacher to presume too early that the pupil has understood the principle of the magic 'e' words. When I first made and used these games, I was surprised to learn how little some pupils had actually grasped. The games became, among other things, an important means of assessment and an interesting way to repeat and practise until the function had been understood. I found that I needed games for

revision for long after the rule had been apparently established. That is why I have devoted a whole book to magic 'e' games.

The games are for anyone who is learning to read and to spell. The deliberate repetition of words and pictures helps the pupils to transfer from the short-term to the long-term memory. They are a tool for teachers who know how important it is but how boring it can be for both pupil and teacher to have to go over the same ground again and again until it is learned. There are many opportunities for talking about words while playing, for inspiring the pupil with the excitement of learning about our English language, and for laughter and enjoyment.

A selection of my magic 'e' games appears in this book. I hope you will use the materials to invent some more games of your own. Even I still enjoy playing the games with my pupils and I have played them all, many times, and proved their worth.

The 'ae' Game

AIMS

○ To draw attention to the 'ae' symbol in words.

○ To help pupils to understand the importance of choosing the correct vowel, in this case 'a' to work with 'e', and to practise reading the words they have made.

HOW TO MAKE THE GAME

○ Cut up the sheets (pages 9 to 11) to make cards that show a picture and an incomplete word. Make small vowel cards with the remaining sheet of vowels (page 12). I suggest that 'a' and 'e' are inked in red, 'i' in blue, 'o' in green, and 'u' in orange.

WHAT YOU NEED

○ A feely bag large enough to contain all the vowel cards.

HOW TO PLAY

○ Give each player three cards showing a picture and an incomplete word. Stack the rest of these cards.

○ Place all the vowel cards in the feely bag.

○ The players take turns to remove one vowel card from the bag. If an 'a' card is drawn, the player may complete one of his picture/word cards, read the word and set it aside, then take a replacement picture/word card from the stack.

○ If the player does not draw an 'a', but gets another vowel instead, this card should not be returned to the bag, but should be put to one side. The game continues until all the cards in the stack have been taken.

○ The winner has the most completed cards.

TEACHER GUIDANCE

I always use this game after I have introduced a pupil to 'magic e'. In my introduction, I write down all five vowels and check that the pupil knows the letter names and the sounds for which the vowels stand. I remind him, briefly, of the three-letter words we have used in which the vowels are 'short', for example 'hat', 'pen', 'pig', 'cot' and 'cup'. I ask how we might spell a word like 'name' and how we would make the 'a' sound like the name of the letter rather than its sound. Pupils sometimes offer ideas. One may try 'ay'. I explain that this does stand for the sound we want, but if we write it in the word 'name' we will not have spelled that word correctly. We will put 'ay' aside and learn about it on another day. If the pupil says, 'Put an "e" on the end', do not be easily misled. You will need to test to find out how much he knows about the function of 'e'.

I write down 'a' and we sound it. I then show how putting an 'e' with it helps the 'a' to stand for its name sound. We demonstrate this by writing about six words that we can make with the help of magic 'e'. I then give the pupil an overview of the effect of magic 'e' on all five vowels. I rub out 'ee', saying, 'We know that one already, "e" is helping itself in words like "tree" and "meet" and "green"'. I then rub out all except 'ae' and explain that these 'ae' words are the ones we are going to look for in our game. 'If you take an "a" out of the bag, you can complete a word, read it to me and keep it on your side of the table.' I sometimes tease them by putting another vowel into the word. We laugh about the non-words and ponder on what a 'snuke' or 'flome' might be! Take every opportunity to demonstrate when 'e' is and is not needed to make the word.

c _ se

fl _ me

c _ ve

sn _ ke

w _ ve

n me	cr ne	pl t e	gr pe	sp de
Jane			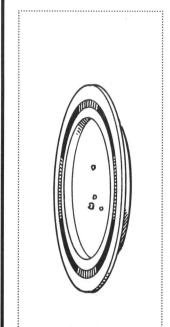	

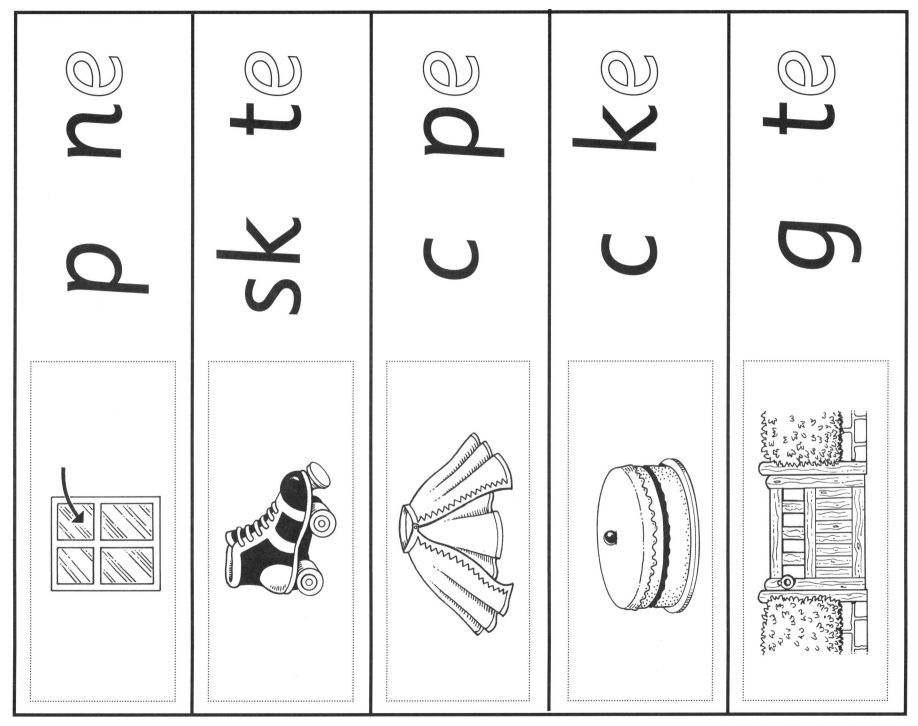

p _ ne

sk _ te

c _ pe

c _ ke

g _ te

o	o	o	o	o
i	i	i	i	i
u	u	u	u	u
a	a	a	a	a
a	a	a	a	a
a	a	a	a	a

'e' or no 'e'? – Game 1

AIMS

❍ To demonstrate how the sound represented by the symbol 'a' is altered when 'e' is added to make 'ae'.

❍ To give opportunity to practise recognising the difference between 'a' words and 'ae' words.

HOW TO MAKE THE GAME

❍ Cut up the picture/word sheets (pages 14 to 17) to make individual cards. Cut off the 'e' pieces and make these into small cards. Extra 'e's have been provided.

WHAT YOU NEED

❍ A die with a green spot on each of five of its sides and a red spot on the sixth side.

❍ A shaking cup.

HOW TO PLAY

❍ Stack the picture/word cards and arrange the small 'e' cards neatly on the table.

❍ Players take turns to throw the die. If a green spot, for 'GO' is thrown, the player may take a card from the top of the stack. (The red spot means 'STOP' and the player who throws it must miss a turn.) He must then decide whether or not his word requires an 'e'. If the word does need an 'e', he should take one, place it appropriately and then set the completed word aside. If the word does not require an 'e', the player keeps the card for himself anyway.

❍ The winner is the person with the most completed cards when all the cards have been used up. Players who either add an 'e' when they should not, or fail to add 'e' when they should, could, at the discretion of the teacher, lose the card, which should be placed at the bottom of the stack.

TEACHER GUIDANCE

The first of these 'e' or no 'e' games deals only with 'ae'. You have taught magic 'e' carefully, possibly in a way I have described in my notes on the 'ae' game (page 8). The pupil has, so far, appeared to understand everything you have said, but in his written work you may have noticed that he has started to put 'e' on everything. You will not be the first teacher to experience an anxious moment! But you have not confused him – he is simply trying out his new skill and fancies that 'e' on everything looks really grown up. You may ask yourself whether it is wrong to teach phonics because it is too hard for pupils to understand, but do not entertain such thoughts! Even while you are thinking them, the pupil's reading vocabulary has increased by hundreds of words and not just by a few words as it is for many pupils who are taught by 'Look and Say'. Experience in writing will soon help him to learn where to put the magic 'e' letters. A good teacher teaches a principle, then teaches it again and again in other, interesting ways, until it is understood.

This game provides the opportunity for the pupil and teacher to see just where there are problems – listen out for the 'messages' in a pupil's hesitation, his misreading a word so that it doesn't describe the picture, or his thoughtfulness in studying the word and picture carefully to decide about the 'e'. These are all indicators of his understanding. Discipline is required, too, as the pupil realises that letters in words and spellings are important. For many pupils, this is a serious, new discovery. 'Look what you've done to "hat". You've made it say "hate" by putting "e" on the end!' This states the problem and for many pupils is the key to sorting out 'e' or no 'e'.

e	e	e	e	e
pan	bag	cap	van	rat

e	e	e	e	e
hat	cas	flam	cav	snak

e	e	e	e	e
gat	cak	wav	skat	pan

e	e	e	e	e
nam	cran	plat	grap	spad
James				

'e' or no 'e'? – Game 2

AIMS

○ To assess the pupil's ability to change over to using the long vowel sounds when they are in conjunction with magic 'e'.

○ To find out how much the pupil understands about this change and to give opportunity to practise the rule.

○ To experience how important 'e' is to the spellings of these words even though it is 'silent'.

HOW TO MAKE THE GAME

○ Cut up the picture/word cards (pages 19 to 22) and separate the 'e's. Extra 'e's are provided.

WHAT YOU NEED

○ A die with green spots on each of the five sides and a red spot on the sixth side.

○ A shaking cup.

HOW TO PLAY

○ Shuffle the picture/word cards and give ten cards to each of the two players. Place the 'e' cards on a pile nearby.

○ Players take turns to shake and throw the die. If green is thrown, the player may consider his top card, as they are all stacked neatly before him, and decide whether or not he needs 'e' for the word to be spelt correctly. He must read the word. If he is right, he should set the card aside, with or without an 'e', as the case may be, then the second player has his turn.

○ Turns must be missed if red is thrown.

○ If a player makes an error, the card must go to the bottom of his pile to be reconsidered later.

○ The first player to work through all his cards is the winner.

TEACHER GUIDANCE

I do not play this game until I have taught 'ae', 'ie', 'oe' and 'ue'.

Older pupils may be interested if you point out to them that, in our lessons so far, we have seen how new sounds can be symbolised by writing two letters together – 'sh', 'ch' and 'th'. In all of the games in this book, however, new sound pictures are made by using 'e' to work with 'a', 'i', 'o' and 'u', although usually they are not written next to one another. The sound 'ae' almost always has a consonant between the 'a' and the 'e'. (I once taught a boy whose name was Daeus.) 'ie' and 'oe' are mainly split apart and 'ee' is rarely split. 'e' can work back over one consonant but not over doubled consonants. I show the pupil some examples of this rule, such as 'din', 'dinner', 'dine', 'diner'; 'bit', 'bitter', 'bite', 'biter'; 'hat', 'hatter', 'hate', 'hater'; 'hop', 'hopper', 'hope', 'hoper'. I tell the pupils that double letters keep the vowel standing for its own sound, but magic 'e' changes the vowel to stand for its name.

'e' can work back over two different consonants, as in 'haste', 'waste' and 'paste, or over a consonant digraph, as in 'bathe', 'blithe' or 'clothe'.

e	e	e	e	e
pot	box	can	tub	jug

e	e	e	e	e
hom	lin	tub	smok	cub

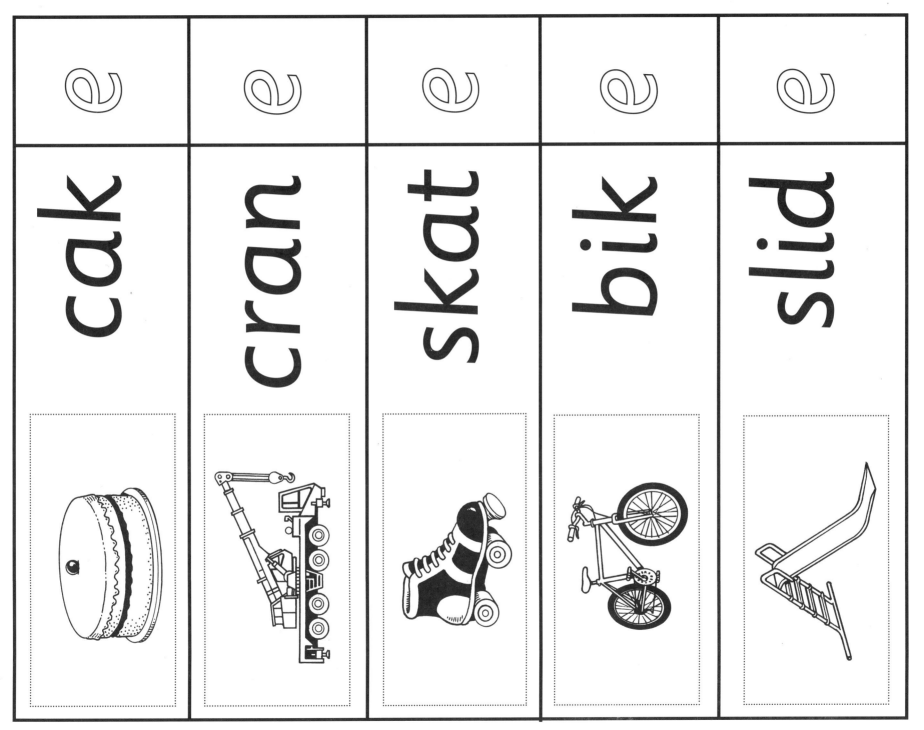

e	e	e	e	e
cak	cran	skat	bik	slid

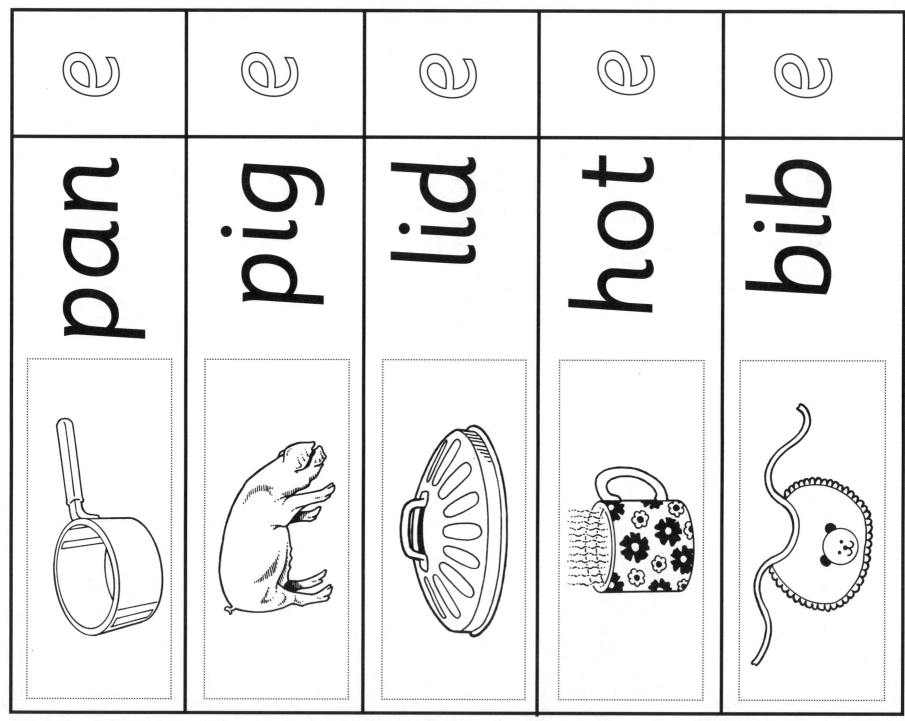

e	e	e	e	e
pan	pig	lid	hot	bib

PHONICABILITY **MAGIC** 'E'

Triplets

AIMS

❍ To focus attention on the combination of 'i' and 'e' making the sound symbol 'ie'.

❍ To help the pupil to hear this sound in words and to read words containing the symbol.

HOW TO MAKE THE GAME

❍ Cut up all the words and pictures (pages 24 to 26) and make them into small cards. Separate the words that belong to the pictures from those that are not illustrated. (I put a small mark on the back of these cards to help with the sorting when the game is being set up.)

HOW TO PLAY

❍ Place the twelve picture cards in a line on the table, face down. Above them, also face down, arrange the row of word cards that belong to the pictures. These should not intentionally be placed above the correct picture.

❍ Above these, place the row of unrelated word cards, word side uppermost. (You can try putting them word side down when you have more time to play the game.)

❍ Players take turns to turn over one picture card and one word card. If these happen to match, they may select a rhyming card from the top row to make a set of three cards. If the selected word card does not belong to the player's picture, it must be replaced in the row and the player must wait for his next turn to try again, keeping the same picture. The rhyming word should be found as soon as the word and picture are paired, and the set of three cards put on the player's side.

❍ The winner is the player with the most sets when all the cards have been used up.

TEACHER GUIDANCE

In addition to focusing on words containing the 'ie' sound, this game gives an opportunity to talk about rhyming words. I usually do this while the pupil is helping me to set up the game. I show him the words 'hide' and 'ride', 'fine' and 'shine', and 'drive' and 'alive', and I tell him that we shall be looking for some words that rhyme with these as we play the game. I point out that the 'ie' sound is the same, but the consonant separating the 'i' and the 'e' may be different, then 'bite' will not rhyme with 'bike'. I show him how the word for 'lie' does not have a consonant between the 'i' and the 'e'. These things may seem very basic, but I have had quite advanced pupils wanting to separate the 'i' and the 'e' and spelling, for example a word like 'tie' as 'tiyee'.

The three rows of cards look a bit daunting at first, but as soon as the search begins the pupil tries to remember where he saw the word for his picture. For this reason, I try to retain the gaps as words cards are removed instead of pushing the cards together. Check as you play that the pupil is sounding the whole word and not just guessing what it is from the initial sound. Guessing is taboo! Pupils with the most insignificant of reading problems soon become proficient in guessing words if they are allowed to do so, as this method seems to them to be a 'short cut'. Do not allow guessing to take root. It is a habit that is very hard to eradicate. If pupils have been trained to depend on trying to recognise words by appearance, but then have to resort to guessing if their memory fails them, the efficiency of learning to read by phonics is spoiled.

like	ripe	fine	smile
ride	lie	bite	alive
strive	drive	shine	hide

tie	dive	line	nine
hive	kite	stile	five
bride	slide	bike	pipe

Focus on 'ue'

AIMS

○ To focus attention on the sound and symbol for 'ue', which many pupils find to be the most difficult of the magic 'e' sounds.

○ To give additional practice in reading magic 'e' words.

HOW TO MAKE THE GAME

○ Cut up all of the words and sounds (pages 28 to 30) to make small cards, then paste the sound symbol 'ue' on the reverse of the 'ue' word cards. The two sheets with three pictures at the top of each (pages 31 and 32) are the boards.

WHAT YOU NEED

○ A dice with 'ae' written on two sides, 'ie' written on two sides and 'oe' written on the remaining two sides.

○ A shaking cup.

HOW TO PLAY

○ Each player has a board. The 'ue' word cards are stored to one side and the other magic 'e' words are spread neatly over the table, word side up.

○ Players take turns to throw the die and take and read a word that contains the sound they have thrown. The word is then placed in the correct column on the player's board. Four words are needed to fill each column.

○ When a player throws a 'sound' for a column that is already filled, he may take and READ a 'ue' word card and, if correct, may keep it.

○ The game continues until one player has filled his board. The winner is the player with the most 'ue' cards.

TEACHER GUIDANCE

When I made this game, I was concerned that so few pupils managed to grasp the 'ue' words as well as they understood 'ae', 'ie' and 'oe'. I have consistently given them only five words to learn for homework, namely 'June', 'rude', 'blue', 'tube' and 'tune' and have explained to them carefully that the 'ue' in 'June', 'rude' and 'blue' sounds different from that in 'tube' and 'tune'. 'In fact,' I say, 'you might want to put "oo" into the words "June", "blue" and "rude" and if you did, everyone would know what you meant, but the spellings would not be right. That is why I want you to be extra careful about remembering that these words are on the "ue" family list.' It would be safe for me to say that none of the pupils I have taught, or teach currently, would be able to spell all the 'ue' words in the game, but I hope, by means of it, to make them more aware of the 'ue' sound and to practise using it as they read the cards. It is a good idea to check that the pupils know the name of the letter 'u'. They sometimes confuse this letter with a 'y'.

This game lends itself to several different versions, according to the age and patience of the pupil. We have, sometimes, had to find the words for all three of our pictures before beginning to fill the columns with words, then use the die to empty them. Sometimes I allow the pupil to add to his score of cards at the end of the game by (accurately) reading 'ue' cards taken from the pile, but not won. I may say, for example, 'If you can read these six words you can keep them.'

shape	save	home
game	plate	smoke
cake	snake	broke
case	rope	rose
gate	bone	joke
made	stone	toe
name	nose	ice

nine	wife	prune
five	shine	tune
time	clue	argue
slide	continue	true
bike	cube	tube
like	flute	blue
line	cute	huge

excuse	ue	ue	ue
rule	ue	ue	ue
glue	ue	ue	ue
use	ue	ue	ue
rude	ue	ue	ue
June	ue	ue	ue
amuse	ue	ue	ue

a . e	**i . e**	**o . e**

a . e	i . e	o . e

Add an 'e', Take an 'e'

AIM

○ To demonstrate the 'magic' of 'e', showing how the meanings of some words are completely altered when the vowel and 'e' work together.

HOW TO MAKE THE GAME

○ Cut up the sheets of words that do not have an 'e' (pages 34 and 35) to make small cards. Keep the sheets of words with 'e' (pages 36 and 37) whole – these are the boards. Use a pen to colour the magic 'e' letters on the boards.

WHAT YOU NEED

○ A bag large enough to contain the small word cards.

HOW TO PLAY

○ Each player has a board of magic 'e' words.

○ The first player takes a word from the bag and reads it aloud, clearly. The second player must examine his board to see if he can match that same word, but changed by a magic 'e'. For example, if the first player draws 'mad', then the second player must look for 'made' on his board. If the second player cannot match the word, it should be placed to one side, on the table, and the second player then draws a word for his partner.

○ Players keep the word cards they have successfully matched, using them to cover the words on their boards.

○ When there are no more cards in the bag, the game could end, with the winner being the player with the most cards on his board. Alternatively, the game could be extended by replacing the rejected cards in the bag and continuing until one player has completely filled his board.

○ Make another game by using the sheets without 'e' for the boards and cutting up the sheets with 'e' to make cards, or use the idea to make a grand 'mix and match' lotto game played with a caller.

TEACHER GUIDANCE

It is difficult for able readers to imagine what mental agility is required by some pupils to change the vowel sound in a word by putting a magic 'e' on the end of it. It is, indeed, a major hurdle for young readers and older pupils who encounter problems with learning to read. Bear that in mind as you play this game. Listen to the pupil as he sounds out the word and translates it into its new meaning. Try not to rush the pupil or prompt too soon. Listen for accurate sounding and blending and point out the wonder of it – that one small letter can so totally alter the meaning of a word.

rip	tap	hid
plum	shin	rob
win	plan	hat
spit	not	cub

can	man	slid
kit	rid	mad
cod	bit	rod
tub	mop	pip

ripe	tape	hide
plume	shine	robe
wine	plane	hate
spite	note	cube

cane	mane	slide
kite	ride	made
code	bite	rode
tube	mope	pipe

Bin It

AIMS

○ To give more experience in hearing the difference between the 'a' sound, as in 'cat', and the 'ae' sound, as in 'fate'.

○ To give practice in making this change quickly in order to speed up reading.

HOW TO MAKE THE GAME

○ Cut up and make individual cards of all the words (pages 39–41). I make my magic 'e's distinctive with a metallic pen.

WHAT YOU NEED

○ A fairly large feely bag to contain all the word cards.

○ Something to use for a 'bin' – I purchased a miniature, plastic dustbin, but a cardboard box would do just as well.

HOW TO PLAY

○ Players take turns to delve into the bag for a word card. They must then read the word correctly.

○ Three-lettered words are thrown into the bin, but magic 'e' words are collected by the players.

○ Words that are incorrectly read should be returned to the bag, but how strict you are depends on the pupil's ability.

○ When the bag is empty, the player with the most magic 'e' words is the winner.

TEACHER GUIDANCE

I do not approve of the verbalisation of nouns, but the pupils' choice of a name for this game seems to have stuck fast.

Make sure as you play, that the pupils do read every word, as in their enthusiasm to collect magic 'e' words they tend to cast the others into the 'bin' carelessly. You will want them to hear the difference between the short and long vowels in 'hat', 'hate'; 'man', 'mane'; 'mad', 'made'; 'cap', 'cape'. Occasionally, I stop the game to consider the meaning of a word, but not often as pupils are impatient of interruptions.

If a word is read incorrectly, put it back into the bag and say something like, 'Let's give that one another chance. You'll be quite sure of it when you see it again.'

bad	tap	hat
map	pat	pan
fan	rag	bag
can	cat	fat
dad	sad	mad

man	ham	cap
wag	jam	bat
rat	name	wake
case	bake	gate
cake	cape	rake

maze	date	cane
tame	save	game
hate	lane	late
came	cave	made
mate	mane	lake

Magic 'e' Lotto

AIMS

○ To give an opportunity to use knowledge of magic 'e' to read some words that may be more demanding than those the pupils have, so far, seen written down.

○ To give opportunities for discussing words and their meanings and for helping pupils to express themselves clearly when defining words.

HOW TO MAKE THE GAME

○ Photocopy both sheets twice (pages 43 and 44). Cut up the second copies (which could be reduced by 25 per cent) to make separate, small cards. Place these word cards into a bag.

WHAT YOU NEED

○ A bag that is large enough to hold the 36 word cards.

HOW TO PLAY

IF A CALLER IS AVAILABLE

○ Give each player a word board.

○ The caller takes a word from the bag and reads it clearly.

○ The player who thinks he has that word on his board must claim it and place it over the same word on the board, matching it carefully to check that he is right.

○ The player whose board is filled first is the winner.

IF YOU ARE PLAYING ONE TO ONE

○ Players draw from the bag for each other.

○ A player must not keep a word he has drawn if his partner does not need it. Instead, the word card must be put to one side.

○ The game proceeds until there are no word cards left in the bag and it can end there, with the winner being the player with the most words covered with cards. Alternatively, the words that have been set aside can be put back in the bag for a second round.

TEACHER GUIDANCE

The 'caller' must be a good reader and on no account should the players see the word that is being called. They should read the words on their cards to see if they have it. This calls for more advanced sounding out skills so be careful not to humiliate the less able pupil by allowing him to play with quicker partners.

The boards can be cut in halves so that four pupils can play and to enlarge the whole set makes it into a very useful game in the classroom setting. It is a popular game and I have sometimes had quite a large group of pupils standing round, watching with great enthusiasm. I encourage observers when appropriate as often they learn as much as the players do! Any teachers or helpers who can spare the time will learn a lot from watching how individual pupils tackle the problem of reading isolated words, that is, words that are not clarified by a supporting text. In my opinion, pupils are not really reading until they can read isolated words.

flame	smoke	glide
shine	price	prune
shame	stole	mute
prize	space	those
stile	stone	plate
scrape	rude	flute

these	trade	smile
blue	place	blame
stride	brake	crime
broke	slope	fuse
duke	stripe	close
brave	huge	globe

Hot Spots

AIM

○ To increase reading skills by means of a crossword game that focuses on magic 'e' words, which are presented downwards as well as across the board.

HOW TO MAKE THE GAME

○ Mount the boards (pages 46 and 47) and join them together so that the top centre word reads 'hive'. Colour the vowels, including those on the boards and those on the separate sheet (page 48), but not the word cards. Colour the hot spots (✳) red. Cut up everything on the letter/word sheet (page 48). Place the vowels and the hot spots into a bag.

WHAT YOU NEED

○ A bag for the vowels and hot spots.

○ A container for the word cards, which enables them to be taken out systematically (a pile may fall over).

○ Some counters (buttons or pebbles will do if you have no posh, coloured ones).

○ A small receptacle for each player in which he may store the counters as they are collected.

HOW TO PLAY

○ Players take turns to draw from the bag.

○ If a vowel is drawn, it must be placed over any similar vowel on the board. If this placing **completes** a word, the player may take one counter from the pool.

○ If a hot spot is drawn, the player may take a word card and, if it is read correctly, he may take two counters and replace the word card in the container, at the back of the pile.

○ When all the vowels are covered, the winner is the player who has the most counters.

TEACHER GUIDANCE

Hot Spots is an old favourite and the first game I made, hoping to solve all the magic 'e' problems I was likely to meet. Such was my ignorance in those days when I did not appreciate the step-by-step nature of the work of teaching phonics. The game still has a place in my programme because being able to read the words down as well as across gives the pupils a sense of achievement. I help them to win by pointing out opportunities although I am often surprised by how soon pupils latch on to the need to complete the words and read them before winning the counter.

If the game has a disadvantage, it is that it takes longer to play than other games. I have sometimes solved this problem by saying, 'We will stop when the big hand of the clock is on … and count up our counters then.'

mile	wipe	blue	stone	slice	true	drove	shake	excuse	close	taste	smile	flute	blame
✳	✳	✳	✳	✳	✳	✳	flame		brave				✳
o	o	o	u	u	u	✳	✳	✳	✳	✳	✳	✳	✳
e	e	i	i	i	i	i	i	i	i	o	o	o	o
e	e	e	e	e	e	e	e	e	e	e	e	e	e
a	a	a	a	a	a	a	a	a	a	a	a	a	a

Listen to magic 'e'

AIM

○ To help pupils to 'hear' the magic 'e' sounds, 'ae', 'ie', 'oe' and 'ue', by looking at the pictures and matching the sound to the symbol on the die.

HOW TO MAKE THE GAME

○ Cut up the picture cards and word cards (pages 51 to 56) and stick the appropriate word on the back of each picture. Ink in the outline letters with the colour of your choice to distinguish the magic 'e' sound in each word.

WHAT YOU NEED

○ A die labelled 'ae', 'ie', 'oe', 'ue', then 'ch' on the fifth side standing for 'choose', and a red spot on the sixth side.

○ A shaking cup.

HOW TO PLAY

○ Arrange the cards picture side up on the table. Neat rows will facilitate easier identification.

○ Players then take turns to shake and throw the die and to take a picture card that has the same sound in its word as that shown on the die.

○ If the red spot is thrown, the player has to miss a turn. If 'ch' is thrown, the player chooses any picture, but must state clearly which sound is in its word.

○ When all cards have been used up, or at the end of a pre-arranged time, the winner is the player with the most cards.

TEACHER GUIDANCE

As you set this spelling game out on the table, talk about the pictures to ensure that the pupils know what they all are. You may need to remove some, such as 'plume' or 'lute', if you feel that your pupils are unlikely to be familiar with these words. However, bear in mind that the vocabularies of older pupils can be increased by discussing the meanings of words, especially if you have a picture to illustrate the meaning. Pupils often 'know' the word, but do not know how to define it or use it in speech, just as very young pupils know what is meant by 'Where is Teddy?', but do not use the words themselves. Draw attention to the arrows that point to the parts of the pictures named on the back – nose, plume, cone and toe. Talk about the words 'house' and 'home'. What is the difference and which word is most likely to be used in a magic 'e' game?

I really get a sense of great satisfaction when I see a pupil tackling this game well. He has to look at the picture, visualise the word and then match what is in his head to the symbol on the die and that could be very difficult. If he makes a mistake, I usually say, 'Are you sure about that? Can you listen to the word in your head again?' I may have to check that the word in his head is indeed the one on the back of the card! If a pupil makes a lot of mistakes, help him for a while and stop the game early. You may have introduced the game too soon and he will need lots more practice with magic 'e' before you go on. Some pupils make mistakes at the beginning of a game while they are getting used to what they have to do, so watch, listen and learn to know exactly where the pupil will need your help next.

Matching Game

AIM

○ To give enjoyment and practice to pupils who are able to read magic 'e' words fairly easily.

HOW TO MAKE THE GAME

○ Cut up both the word cards and the picture cards (pages 51 to 56). Place the word cards in a bag (they may be reduced in size for this game).

WHAT YOU NEED

○ A feely bag.

○ A die marked 1 on two sides, 2 on two sides, and 3 on two sides.

○ A shaking cup.

HOW TO PLAY

○ Arrange the picture cards on the table so that they can be viewed easily.

○ Players take turns to throw the die and draw word cards from the bag according to the number shown on the die. These words must then be read and matched to the appropriate picture card(s).

○ The game continues either until all the cards are used up, or the agreed time limit set for the game has expired.

○ The winner is the player with the most pairs.

TEACHER GUIDANCE

This is essentially a reading game; it is very simple to play and can be timed to suit your programme. I play it with pupils who need practice in reading the magic 'e' words after we have studied 'ae', 'ie', 'oe' and 'ue'.

People love collecting things and a good pile of something pleases them, especially if they have won the things they have collected. Exactly how the pupils cope with the multiplicity of words and pictures indicates to me how quickly they are processing the words and are able to choose the right ones from among so many.

We talk about the pictures as we set them out in rows to aid systematic search, but because reading the words on the cards is the most important activity, I am happy to help when one asks, 'Lute… What's a lute, Miss?'

A more demanding version of the game can be played by placing all the picture cards in the bag and lining up the word cards on the table. If a pupil hesitates too long over finding the word, check that he is looking for the word that describes the picture – 'chimney' for 'smoke' for example. Do not prolong either of these games if you feel that the pupil is out of his depth, as the sense of achievement lies in being able to accrue a lot of pairs in as short a time as possible.

tune	tube	cube
lute	plume	rose
rope	toe	smoke
cone	home	nose

PHONICABILITY **MAGIC** 'E'

pipe	tie	five
nine	skate	gate
cake	plate	crane
case	snake	name

PHONICABILITY **MAGIC 'E'**

note	dome	hole
sole	bride	slide
dive	stile	line
bike	kite	hive

PHONICABILITY MAGIC 'E'